100 Questions and Answers About American Jews with a Guide to Jewish Holidays

Michigan State University
School of Journalism

Read The Spirit Books

an imprint of
David Crumm Media, LLC
Canton, Michigan

For more information and further discussion, visit

http://news.jrn.msu.edu/culturalcompetence/

Cover art and design by
Rick Nease
www.RickNeaseArt.com

Published By
Read The Spirit Books
an imprint of
David Crumm Media, LLC
42015 Ford Rd., Suite 234
Canton, Michigan, USA

For information about customized editions, bulk purchases or permissions, contact David Crumm Media, LLC at info@DavidCrummMedia.com

Contents

Acknowledgments

Michigan State University students who wrote this guide, from left: Daniel Hamburg, Lia Kamana, David Reiss, Tiara Jones, Darren Weiss, Gabriela Saldivia, Nathaniel Strauss, Madeline Carino, Riccardo Cozzolino, Kary Moyer, Isaac Berkowitz and Katie Krall.

We are especially grateful to **Allan Gale**, associate director at the Detroit Jewish Community Relations Council. He proposed this guide many years ago, advised the early planning and every stage of the editing, and met with the class.

The following people helped edit the questions and the answers. They helped ensure the guide's accuracy and authority.

Kari Alterman is a senior program officer with the William Davidson Foundation. From 2007 to 2015, Alterman served as the Detroit regional director for the American Jewish Committee. Prior to joining

AJC, Alterman spent 11 years working with the Jewish Federation of Metropolitan Detroit. She has also served with the Detroit Jewish News Foundation and the InterFaith Leadership Council of Metropolitan Detroit.

Wendy Rose Bice is director of the Jewish Historical Society of Michigan and editor of Michigan Jewish History.

Rabbi Amy B. Bigman has served Congregation Shaarey Zedek, East Lansing, Michigan, since 2007. Earlier service includes the board and then assistant director of the Ecumenical Institute for Jewish-Christian Studies in Southfield, Michigan; the advisory committee of the Jewish Experiences for Families in Southfield, Michigan; and the parent curriculum committee for the Michigan Jewish AIDS Coalition. She also served two years as the president of the Association of Reform Rabbis of Greater St. Louis. As a member of the Religious Coalition for Reproductive Choice's Clergy Institute she gave a briefing on Capitol Hill. She hosted this guide's authors at Shaarey Zedek.

Rabbi Azaryah Moshe Cohen is Head of School at The Jean and Samuel Frankel Jewish Academy of Metropolitan Detroit. It is a high school "built upon a dual curriculum of the highest-level college preparatory general studies and classical text-based Jewish studies while operating within a framework of Jewish law."

David Crumm is co-founder of David Crumm Media LLC and Front Edge Publishing, as well as ReadTheSpirit online magazine and publishing house. He has advised this series from its roots in the late 1990s when he was the long-time religion writer at the Detroit Free Press. For this guide, he edited the religious holidays section.

Arthur Horwitz is founder and president of the Detroit Jewish News Foundation. He is also president and publisher of Renaissance Media/The Detroit Jewish News. Horwitz has also been chosen for the boards of trustees and board chairmanships with the Michigan Civil Rights Commission and Detroit Public TV.

Gail Katz is co-founder of WISDOM (Women's Interfaith Solutions for Dialogue and Outreach in MetroDetroit). She is also education committee chair of the InterFaith Leadership Council of Metropolitan Detroit.

Doron Levin is a contributor to Fortune magazine, Fortune.com and TheStreet.com. He has been a reporter and columnist with Bloomberg News, the Detroit Free Press and The New York Times.

Bobbie Lewis is a contributing writer for The Detroit Jewish News, an editor and one-time nonprofit communicator who blogs about food.

Joe Lewis' Singlish Publication Society's books of Jewish prayer transliterate Hebrew into modern English to remove barriers to participation.

Judy Loebl is director of adult Jewish learning for the Jewish Federation of Metropolitan Detroit. She has been involved in Jewish education for more than 40 years. Loebl was director of Congregation T'Chiyah Sunday School; developed and directed the Grosse Pointe Jewish Community Council Sunday School and served as director of special programs/educational consultant for the Agency for Jewish Education. She also taught for the Community Jewish High School; served as principal of the Community Jewish High School/director of teen education for the Agency for Jewish Education; and was an instructor of Jewish and Israeli literature at the Midrasha College of Jewish Studies. Prior to her current position, Loebl was director of SAJE (Seminars for Adult Jewish Enrichment) for the Jewish Community Center.

Howard Lupovitch is director of the Cohn-Haddow Center for Jewish Studies at Wayne State University. He serves as Congregation Beth Ahm's regular Torah reader.

Deborah Margolis is librarian for Middle East Studies & Anthropology at Michigan State University Libraries. She is liaison to the Anthropology Department, Jewish Studies Program and the Muslim Studies Program. She read a draft of the guide and contributed to the resources section.

Zlati Meyer is a reporter with the Detroit Free Press. She has also reported for the Philadelphia Inquirer and United Press International.

Barbara Raab is a program officer with the Ford Foundation and an adjunct associate professor at the CUNY Graduate School of Journalism. She previously was a senior newswriter and a senior member of the editorial leadership team at NBC News.

Rabbi Steven Rubenstein has served Congregation Beth Ahm, West Bloomfield, Michigan, since 2007. He served as the associate rabbi of Congregation Beth Shalom in Kansas City, Missouri, from 2000-2005 and has been president of the Michigan Region of the Rabbinical Assembly and an officer of the Interfaith Health & Hope Coalition.

Sheri Schiff is an anti-bias and multi-cultural educator, a docent at the Holocaust Memorial Center in Farmington Hills, Michigan, and part of the force behind Bookstock and WISDOM. She is a board member of the American Jewish Committee and other Jewish organizations.

Meredith Skowronski is administrator with the InterFaith Leadership Council of Metropolitan Detroit.

Rabbi Daniel B. Syme serves Temple Beth El of Bloomfield Hills, Michigan. He is former senior vice president of the Union for Reform Judaism and author of 24 books, including "The Jewish Home: A Guide for Jewish Living" and "100 Books for Jewish Readers." Service has included vice president of the American Zionist Youth Movement and the American Zionist Movement. He has been director-at-large of the board of the Jewish National Fund of America and a board member of the United Israel Appeal. He chaired the Coalition for the Advancement of Jewish Education and held board or leadership positions with the Memorial Foundation for Jewish Culture, the National Council for Jewish Education, the Ecumenical Institute and the Coalition for Jewish Unity.

We are also grateful for the advice of Cindy Hughey, executive director of Michigan State University Hillel and the MSU Hillel Foundation. She encouraged the project, fed some of us and opened the Lester and Jewell Morris Jewish Student Center to us. We received helpful direction from Yael S. Aronoff, director of the Jewish Studies Program and the Michael and Elaine Serling and Friends Chair of Israel Studies at Michigan State University. Finally, thanks to Lucinda Davenport, professor and director of the School of Journalism in Michigan State's College of Communication Arts and Sciences, for her support of this series.

Foreword

By Rabbi Bob Alper

There's a great old story about how two angry congregants came to their rabbi's home, one by one, to present their sides of a long-simmering dispute.

After hearing the first, the rabbi offered, "You know. I think you're right." Later, the second man appeared and stated his side of the dispute, to which the rabbi replied, "You know. I think you're right."

The rabbi's wife had listened to both discussions from an adjoining room, and when they were alone, she said to her husband, "You told the first man he was right. And you told the second man he was right. They both can't be right."

The rabbi thought for a moment, nodded his head, and responded, "You know, I think you're right."

The term "laconic Jew" is, to me, an oxymoron. We are a highly opinionated people, in love with language, with a healthy addiction to argumentation, verbal wordplay, parsing of terms and, yes, comedy, with its dependence on skillful editing. Thus, the apt phrase, "When there are two Jews, there are three opinions." Our love for intellectual jousting is, no doubt, one of the keys to our long survival.

Into this almost genetically disputatious community stepped Michigan State's School of Journalism, daring, and succeeding well, to address 100 questions about Jewish Americans. It did so by means of clear, informative and understandable responses with which many, but oh, definitely not all Jews, will agree. That would be totally out of character!

And there you have, with a smile, description Number 101 of American Jews.

Rabbi Bob Alper served congregations for 14 years and holds a doctorate from Princeton Theological Seminary. He is also a stand-up comedian and author. Alper performs at corporate events, theaters, non-profits, conventions, private parties, churches and synagogues. In addition to being a full-time stand-up comic and conducting annual High Holy Days services, Alper is the author of three books: "Life Doesn't Get Any Better Than This," the award-winning full-color cartoon book "A Rabbi Confesses" and "Thanks. I Needed That."

Introduction

By Kirsten Fermaglich

This brief guide introduces readers to the religion, culture, politics, demographics and history of Jews in the United States.

As the text rightly emphasizes, there is no one narrative of Jews in America. Jews are a diverse group, who differ in their gender, ethnicity, race, sexuality, age, religious affiliation, politics and region. And Jews further differ in their understandings of what it means to be a Jew: Is it a religion or is it an ethnic group? It is difficult to create one narrative story out of these different threads.

Yet, by asking a diverse set of questions—many of them questions that I have heard from my students or friends—this book offers readers an introduction to some of the most important basic facts that they might need to explore American Jewish life further. As one of the two largest populations of Jews in the world, and as central participants in American culture and society, American Jews are an important group to understand.

Although some may assume that the American Jewish population is fairly new, the community dates back to 1654. Long before the incorporation of the United States, 23 refugees from the Spanish Inquisition, as it moved to Brazil from Portugal, sought asylum in what was then New Amsterdam (and later became New York). As relatively segregated and despised outsiders in Europe, Jews' permission to reside in the European colonies of North America was by no means guaranteed. Yet, these refugees were ultimately allowed to stay in New Amsterdam and become a part of the fabric of the colony and then the emerging nation. The ability of the fledgling United States to incorporate and tolerate Jews as white citizens—despite many political inequities that they initially faced—marked a significant difference between the United States and Europe and suggested the possibility that Jews might be included as equals in the new nation.

The Jewish population of the United States remained small, however, until industrialization in the 19th century provoked waves of migration from throughout the world. As traditional employment for Jews faltered, and as they faced increasing persecution first in Germany, then in Eastern Europe, especially Russia, Jews migrated to the United States seeking both employment and tolerance. The construction of the railroad in the middle of the 19th century provided transportation for Jews with long histories of peddling to establish themselves as salesmen and shopkeepers throughout the hinterland. By the late 19th and early 20th centuries, the industrialization of the clothing industry brought hundreds of thousands of Jews, with backgrounds as tailors and seamstresses, work in Boston, Chicago and New York sweatshops making cheap, ready-to-wear clothing. In 1820, the Jewish population of the United States was roughly 5,000; by 1920, it was 1.6 million.

As Jews entered the United States in large numbers, they built communal life while struggling to adjust to a new, Christian culture. Their religious precepts—abstaining from all work on the Sabbath, eating kosher food—were difficult to follow in an integrated society, particularly as poverty stalked newcomers' existence. When Jews had lived in segregated Jewish communities in Europe, fulfilling all the requirements of their religion had been easier. But in both the small towns of the American Midwest and the crowded city streets of New York, Jewish immigrants found that it was possible and indeed easy to change their religious customs to integrate into American society. Different groups of Jews embraced different methods of integration. Some turned to Reform Judaism, a religious movement that embraced monotheism, but abandoned many Jewish rituals in an effort to highlight the similarities between Jews and Christians. Others turned to Conservative Judaism in an effort to maintain some of the most meaningful Jewish rituals, while still embracing the English language and American culture. Still other Jews abandoned religion altogether and embraced secular Jewish identities, focusing on language, culture, theater and art.

In addition to religious life, Jews built a host of other institutions: fraternal societies, defense organizations, community centers, charities, unions and women's organizations, to name just a few examples. Jews also became increasingly a part of the country's political and cultural life. Women joined national organizations for suffrage, birth control and peace; men joined political parties, voted and joined civic organizations. In many ways, Jews constructed an American life much like that of many other Americans by the 20th century.

Yet, as increasing numbers of Jews entered the country, there was growing unease among wealthy and elite Americans about Jewish cultural, religious and perceived racial differences. Elite hotels, colleges and businesses began to limit Jewish visitors, students and employees, sometimes very openly and publicly pronouncing the incompatibility of Jews with their institutions. The rise of this institutionalized anti-Semitism—part of a trend toward scientific racism at the time—led to new laws in the 1920s that sharply limited immigration from Southern and Eastern Europe for the next 40 years. With no new Yiddish-speaking Orthodox Jews immigrating from Eastern Europe, the American Jewish community became even more integrated into American life than it had been before. American born, English-speaking Jews moved beyond their parents' sweatshop jobs, and integrated into the middle class as secretaries, teachers and small-business owners. They also helped to establish new industries in popular culture, such as film and music. Yet, their comfortable lives in the urban middle class were still fundamentally pursued in Jewish neighborhoods and workplaces. Institutionalized anti-Semitism limited their opportunities, occasionally exposed them to violence and made them uneasy about their ability to fully integrate into America.

And that anti-Semitism lingered into the years after World War II. Immigration restrictions remained tight, making it difficult for Holocaust survivors to come to the country after World War II until years after the war. Elite colleges' quotas limiting Jewish students remained until the 1960s. Yet, at the same time, the postwar boom and the civil rights activism of Jews themselves helped to fundamentally improve American Jews' economic and social integration into American life. Jewish defense organizations worked together with African-American organizations like the NAACP to create civil rights legislation that, by the 1960s, had mostly eliminated barriers to Jewish employment and education, as well as Jim Crow segregation.

In the years after the 1960s, Jews became increasingly prosperous members of the American middle class. They moved into suburban neighborhoods and intermarried with non-Jews at high rates. Yet they also became more vocal in expressing themselves as Jews. Jewish political organizations turned inward, focusing on movements to aid Soviet Jewry and to support Israel in the Middle East. American Jewish artists like Phillip Roth, Barbra Streisand and Woody Allen made American Jewish experiences more visible than they had previously been to non-Jews. And after years of seeming moribund in America, Orthodox Judaism expanded greatly and it became a visible force in the American religious landscape. In the new millennium, Jews are able to participate fully in American life, while openly exhibiting their Jewishness in American culture, politics and religion.

Kirsten Fermaglich is associate professor of history and Jewish Studies at Michigan State University. Her book on American social scientists and Holocaust metaphors, "American Dreams and Nazi Nightmares: Early Holocaust Consciousness and Liberal America, 1957-1965," appeared in 2006. She is also co-editor (with Lisa Fine) of the Norton Critical Edition of Betty Friedan's "The Feminine Mystique" (2013). She has published in the Journal of American Ethnic History, American Jewish History, the Michigan Historical Review, and several edited collections. Currently, she is researching the history of Jewish people and name changing in the 20th century for a book tentatively titled "A Rosenberg by Any Other Name."

About this Guide

The Michigan State University School of Journalism designed this series as a journalistic tool to replace bias and stereotype with accurate information. We create guides that are factual, clear and accessible.

Questioning and dialogue are deeply ingrained in Jewish tradition, beginning with the study of scriptural texts. Questioning keeps Judaism alive and relevant in changing times. Questions are also central to journalism. We began this guide by asking dozens of Jewish people with different perspectives and practices what they thought people wanted or needed to know about them. Some questions are simple, but the answers seldom are. A full discussion would fill volumes. It is also reasonable to ask whether these are even the right questions.

One of the last questions we took up, even after the cover had been designed, was whether the title should refer to "American Jews" or "Jewish Americans." It might seem like a simple question. But it is not. There are strongly held views, well supported, for both labels. And labels are a simplistic way to describe the complexity of a people. We made the best choice we could for the cover, based on the discussion, but we use both terms inside to recognize that opinions vary.

Finally, we know there can be no universally satisfactory set of such questions. We hope you will consider these as a place to start.

Here, then, we present an imperfect introduction to American Jews. Have the conversations the questions should engender. Use the resources we include. Understanding does not come from one small guide or from one conversation, but from an ongoing discussion and asking more questions.

Guide editor
Susan Goldberg, editor-in-chief of National Geographic Magazine and editorial director for National Geographic Partners

Series editor
Joe Grimm, visiting editor in residence, Michigan State University School of Journalism
joe.grimm@gmail.com

Identity

1 Are Jews a religion, race, ethnicity, nationality, culture or a people?

Jews are all of these. They are a people with a shared religion, history, present and future. Most Jewish people observe religious aspects of Judaism to some degree. They share a common culture. It includes literature, art, music, dance and theater, as well as traditions involving language and food. Jewish people generally support remembrance of the Holocaust and the sovereignty of the modern State of Israel, though opinions diverge on its policies. While there are genetic similarities among some Jewish people, there are Jews from all ethnicities, nationalities and racial groups.

2 What is the Jewish Diaspora?

Diaspora means dispersion from a shared homeland and the dislocation that implies. Jews who live outside present-day Israel are considered part of this Diaspora. The Diaspora began with the Babylonian destruction of the First Temple in 586 Before Common Era. Forced and voluntary movements followed. Some people were scattered by conquest, enslaved, driven to new lands, and then persecuted and murdered. Others emigrated to find religious freedom or opportunities and made fortunes in shipping, other forms of trade and the professions. The Jewish Diaspora covers the world.

3 If people convert to Judaism, are they accepted as being Jewish?

Each denomination has a different conversion process. People who become Jewish by choice are full members of the communities they join. It is against Jewish tradition to treat them as outsiders. However, not all streams of Judaism accept conversions by other streams of Judaism.

4 How does one convert to Judaism?

It is important to first state that Jews do not seek converts. People who become Jewish by choice initiate their conversions. The process varies depending on the branch of Judaism (major ones are Reform, Conservative, Reconstructionist and Orthodox). It typically begins by talking with a rabbi. Steps can include studying Judaism, formally accepting Jewish rituals and tradition, meeting with a Religious Court, becoming circumcised, immersion in a ritual bath, choosing a Hebrew name and being welcomed into the community.

5 Are all Jewish people ritually observant?

No, many connect through culture, food or family, but do not affiliate with a religious community and rarely engage in religious rites. They might be Jewish by background or affinity and identify as secular or cultural Jews. They might be deeply religious, or not.

6 What are differences between Sephardic and Ashkenazic Jews?

The terms describe place of origin, tradition and mentality. Ashkenazic Jews have roots in Eastern, Central and parts of Western Europe. Sephardic Jews originally lived in the region of Spain and Portugal. Many Sephardic Jews migrated to Northern Africa after they were expelled from Spain in 1492. The term includes some Jews from Western Asia, Greece, the Middle East and colonies of Spain and Portugal who observed Sephardic interpretations of Jewish law or customs. Mizrachic Jews have roots in the Middle East or Northern Africa. These distinctions, with different worship, food and cultural traditions, are more pronounced in Israel than in the United States. The vast majority of American Jews have Ashkenazic roots. In Hebrew, Ashkenazi refers to Germany, Sephardi to Spain, and Mizrachi to eastern.

Religion

7 What do we call the Jewish religion?

The religion of the Jewish people is Judaism.

8 How did Judaism begin?

The Jewish people and Judaism began at different times. Jews trace their ancestry as a nation of people back about 4,000 years to Abraham, his wife, Sarah, and their son Isaac and grandson Jacob. Abraham, a Hebrew man who lived circa 2000-1800 Before Common Era in Babylon, is the father of the Jewish religion. Going against prevailing religions, Abraham believed that all creation was the work of just one God. Judaism was the world's first major monotheistic religion. The Hebrew scriptures recount that God gave Abraham's descendants special responsibilities and a homeland. The start of Judaism as a religion dates to about 1400 Before Common Era at Mount Sinai. That is where the Israelites received the Ten Commandments, or utterances, and the basis of Hebrew scriptures, the Torah.

9 What is the Torah?

The Torah holds the foundational scriptures of Judaism. The Torah, also called the Pentateuch, is the first five books of the Tanakh. They are Genesis, Exodus, Leviticus, Numbers and Deuteronomy. These are also called the five books of Moses. The Torah includes 613 commandments. The Torah is part of the Hebrew scriptures, but the word is sometimes used to refer to the entire Hebrew Bible.

View video at: http://bit.ly/1Rj770p

10 What is the Tanakh?

This is the Hebrew Bible. Tanakh comes from the acronym for the Hebrew words describing the three major sections: Torah, Prophets (Joshua, Judges, Isaiah, etc.) and Writings (Psalms, Proverbs and more.) The Tanakh has great variety, describing history, culture, laws, ethical teachings, writings and advice. The Christian Old Testament is similar, but in a different order. Hebrew Bible and Tanakh are more theologically neutral terms than "Old Testament." That can imply the replacement theology notion of "Old and outdated" versus "New and improved."

11 What is the Talmud?

The Talmud, codified around 500 Common Era, is a commentary on the Torah and the commandments. It interprets Judaic law. It uses teachings from many rabbis that most observant Jews follow today for living a happy and healthy life. The Talmud, largely in Aramaic, also contains narratives and stories.

12 What does it mean to be "God's chosen people?"

This phrase is mentioned several times in the Torah. It has frequently been misunderstood. It has also been misconstrued to promote anti-Semitism. It means that the Jewish people have accepted special responsibilities and obligations to others because of a contract and partnership with God. This does not mean Jews are better than others, and not all streams of Judaism accept the idea of chosenness.

13 What is the difference between a rabbi and a cantor?

Rabbi is the Hebrew word for "my teacher." Rabbis teach through sermons, classes and in other ways. The rabbi is the religious leader of a congregation and prepares a weekly speech or sermon, advises congregants and often represents the congregation to the community. A cantor, or chazzan, sings or chants liturgical prayers and serves as a leader, teacher and pastor. To become a rabbi, one must go to rabbinical school and study for four to eight years. This can also be accomplished, especially in the Orthodox community, through intensive individual study with a respected rabbi. Some rabbinic students are required to complete a thesis and, after a lengthy period of service, can receive a doctoral degree. Advanced training is also required of cantors. This focuses on learning prayers, vocal performance and leading services. Traditionally, prayers during services are chanted in Hebrew.

14 Why do some Jewish people not drive, use electricity or engage in certain other activities on Shabbat?

Shabbat, the Hebrew word for Sabbath, recalls how God took a day of rest after six days of creating the world. The commandments tell people to take a day of rest, too. Traditionally, rest means cessation from specific creative activities outlined in the Mishna and Talmud. Contemporary rabbis determine what modern activities would be violations of ancient principles. Most American Jews do not observe Shabbat in a strictly traditional way. For those who do, that can mean no work, cooking, spending money, using electronic devices or writing. There is a wide spectrum of how Jewish people celebrate Shabbat. Shabbat begins at sundown on Friday and continues until sundown on Saturday.

15 Why are there so many Jewish holidays from work or school?

This seems so for several reasons. For one, American schools and many workplaces accommodate Christian holidays such as Christmas and Easter, sometimes closing for days, but they don't close for Jewish holidays. This can make Jewish holidays seem "extra." Because Jewish holidays come at varying days on the secular calendar, they surprise people. Also, Jewish days run from sundown to sundown. This means the Sabbath and holidays occupy parts of two generic days. Holidays when many Orthodox and some Conservative or traditional Jews refrain from work are the High Holidays of Rosh Hashanah and Yom Kippur and the pilgrimage holidays of Passover, Shavuot and Sukkot. During Passover and Sukkot, work may be performed during the intermediary days. However, some Orthodox Jews refrain from certain types of work even on those days. On fast days, especially the ninth of Av, many Orthodox Jews refrain from work and play so they may focus on fasting and repentance. These and other holidays are described in a section near the end of this guide.

16 What are the major branches of Judaism?

- The most stringent branch of Judaism is Orthodox Judaism. It emphasizes observance of both the moral obligations and practices of Jewish law. Orthodoxy holds the 613 biblical commandments as binding. Numerous rabbinic enactments and decrees are considered binding, as well. This is called Jewish law, or the halakha.

- Reform Judaism holds ethical laws as binding, while adapting practices to fit the modern world. Reform Jews view Judaism's essence as morality and social justice, while encouraging individuals to maintain practices they find meaningful. They favor individual choice over obligatory beliefs and practices.

- Conservative Judaism developed mainly in the late 19th century as a reaction to Reform Judaism's liberalism. It later assumed its separate identity. Conservative Judaism seeks to preserve traditional observance while allowing for adaptation to contemporary American life. It is a middle ground between Orthodox and Reform.

- The Reconstructionist Movement started as a movement within Conservative Judaism in the mid 20th century. Within Reconstructionist Judaism, Jewish law is a guide that strengthens community, but it is not binding.

- Hasidism is a branch of Orthodox Judaism that includes the Chabad (Lubavitch) movement and many other branches and dates to 18th century Eastern Europe. Hasidic men often wear black jackets or coats, pants, hats and shoes with white shirts. They also wear their hair with uncut sidelocks and wear beards. Women traditionally keep arms, legs and hair covered.
- Jewish Renewal seeks to restore the spiritual vitality and viability of the 19th century Hasidic movement. A transdenominational movement, it holds that Judaism is an evolving religious civilization. It is based in the prophetic and mystical traditions of Judaism.
- Humanistic Judaism began in the 1960s. It emphasizes Jewish tradition, culture, ethics, values and relationships over God. Some members of Humanist congregations consider themselves to be atheists.
- Modern Orthodox Judaism, or Modern Orthodoxy, embraces traditional Jewish practices and encourages full engagement in the secular world. It teaches that engagement in the larger community increases opportunities to foster goodness.

How do American Jews identify religiously?

According to one of the most comprehensive and wide-scale studies of American Jews by the Pew Research Center in 2013, a majority of self-identified Jews claimed that being Jewish is mostly about ancestry and culture, rather than the religious practice of Judaism. While 62 percent of Jews say that being Jewish is more about ancestry and culture, 15 percent said it's about religious belief. For those who do identify as observant Jews, here is the rundown on how they declare their denomination:

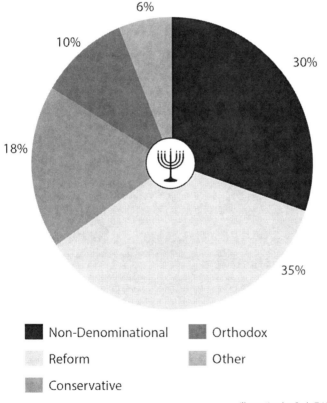

Non-Denominational   Orthodox

Reform   Other

Conservative

illustration by Cody T. Harrell
source: Pew Research Center, 2013

17 How many synagogues are in the United States?

An American Jewish Committee census of synagogues in 2002 found 3,727. Forty percent were Orthodox, and they tended to be smaller. Reform synagogues made up 28 percent of all synagogues. Conservative synagogues comprised 23 percent. Other denominations each had fewer than 3 percent of the total. Some synagogues offer services in more than one denomination. Although they may be part of national or international religious bodies, synagogues are autonomous. Jewish people do not need to pray in a specific type of synagogue.

18 Can non-Jews attend Jewish services?

Non-Jews are typically welcome in most synagogues and to join some parts of the services.

19 How are Judaism, Christianity and Islam alike?

These religions are all monotheistic, meaning they teach there is only one God. Judaism is the oldest of the three. Islam is the newest. These religions are called the Abrahamic religions because all view Abraham as their patriarch and a major prophet. Shared scriptural foundations have created some similar practices and scriptural uses.

In what ways do Americans identify as Jewish?

When Pew Research researched what factors affected how American Jews consider themselves Jewish, they broke the general population into two categories: Jews by background and by affinity. Jews by background were either raised Jewish or had a Jewish parent, but they may not identify religiously as Jewish. Jews by affinity may or may not have been born into a Jewish family, but they identify as Jewish or partially Jewish through religion and observation of Jewish holidays. They asked each population what they considered to be the most important factor when self-identifying as Jewish.

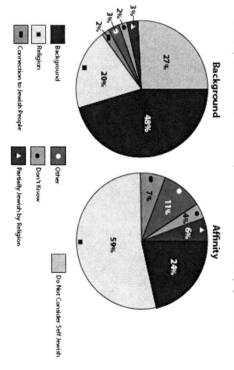

Background

- 27%
- 48%
- 20%
- 3%
- 2%
- 3%
- 3%
- 2%

Affinity

- 59%
- 24%
- 7%
- 11%
- 6%

Legend:
- Background
- Religion
- Connection to Jewish People
- Other
- Don't Know
- Partially Jewish by Religion
- Do Not Consider Self Jewish

20 How are Judaism, Christianity and Islam different?

There are many differences in beliefs, practices, traditions, structure, texts and calendars. There are also different understandings of God's role in people's lives and practices. A chief difference has to do with the role of Jesus. Jews do not believe Jesus was God, as Christians do, or a prophet, as Muslims do. Christians believe Jesus was the messiah. Jews and Muslims do not.

21 Who are Jews for Jesus?

The beliefs of this group align more with Christianity than with Judaism. Members believe Jesus was the messiah. Jews for Jesus recruit Jewish people to join them. Their beliefs and practices are not part of any Jewish traditions, streams or movements. Mainstream Jews do not consider them to be Jewish.

History

22 How long have Jewish people lived in the United States?

Jewish immigration to the United States can be divided into four waves.

- The first wave began in 1654 when Jewish people came from Recife, Brazil, to New Amsterdam, later New York. This group came primarily to seaports as traders.

- The second wave, starting around 1820, is often referred to as the "German wave." Jewish people left Germany and other parts of Western Europe because of persecution, restrictive laws, economic hardship, and the failure of religious reform. They settled in many cities and established national Jewish organizations that exist today.

- After 1880, most Jewish immigrants came from Eastern Europe including Russia, Poland, Austria-Hungary and Romania. They sought financial and social advancement. They were fleeing oppression and poverty.

- Starting in 1945, Jews came as refugees from the Holocaust, the Middle East and the Soviet

Union. Some left one country and lived in others before settling in the United States.

23 What is the Jewish leadership structure?

Judaism does not have a world leader like a pope, and American Jews do not have a top leader, as some nations do. Major U.S. Jewish organizations do have a council of presidents. Major streams of Judaism have bodies that set standards, including how congregations engage with their rabbis and other clergy. Congregations and communities are the building blocks of Jewish leadership.

24 What have been the major Jewish population centers around the world?

There are approximately 13 million to 14 million Jewish people in the world. They make up 0.2 percent of the world's population. More than 80 percent of the world's Jewish population lives in Israel and the United States. Other countries, including Russia, France, Canada, Argentina, the United Kingdom, Germany, South Africa and Hungary, also have sizeable Jewish populations. Almost every country in Europe has a Jewish community and there are remnants of communities in the Middle East. The Holocaust decimated Europe's Jewish population. According to the American Jewish Year Book,

Europe had about 9.5 million Jewish people in 1933 and only 3.5 million in 1950. Poland, which had more than 3 million Jews in 1933, had only 45,000 in 1950. Before the Holocaust, 60 percent of all Jewish people lived in Europe. In 1950, more than half lived in North and South America. Jewish communities are growing today in parts of Asia, Australia and Latin America.

Language

25 What is the language of Jewish prayer and the Torah?

The classical, sacred language of Jewish prayer and the Torah is Hebrew. However, prayers may be said in other languages.

26 Is the Hebrew in the Torah the same as spoken Hebrew?

No. Hebrew is an ancient language and, like others, has changed over time. Jewish scriptures vary according to when they were written. As a language of daily use, it ebbed and flowed and largely disappeared around 200-400 Common Era. Modern Hebrew, spoken and written, was largely the result of the efforts of lexicographer Eliezer Ben Yehuda in the late 1800s. With immigrants to Israel speaking dozens of languages, Modern Hebrew stitched the new society together and linked communities around the world.

27 What is the difference between Hebrew and Yiddish?

Hebrew is the primary Jewish language and the official language of Israel. Yiddish, the historical language of Ashkenazic Jews, was once the language most widely used by Jewish people. Yiddish derives from Hebrew and Middle High German but has its own grammar. Written Yiddish uses Hebrew characters. If someone asks, "Do you speak Jewish?" they probably mean Yiddish. Many Orthodox Jews speak Yiddish.

28 Are there other Jewish languages?

There are several Jewish languages and dialects, as Jews adapted speech and writing to their local communities. One is Ladino, or Judeo-Spanish. This is the Spanish-Jewish dialect spoken by Sephardic Jews. It comes from Old Spanish and was used both in Spain and the Ottoman Empire. It is a minority language in dozens of countries. Another is Judeo-Arabic, a spoken and written adaptation of Arabic. There are others.

29 Why do we see the same word differently, like matzah, matza, matzoh?

Varying pronunciations and styles of transliterating Hebrew lead to variations in English. The Hebrew alphabet is 22 consonants and indicates vowels with small marks, called vowel points. These are above, beneath or beside the consonants. When Hebrew is brought into English, vowels are written as letters.

30 What is the guttural sound used in Hebrew?

This sound, which is not pronounced in English, is spelled as either ch, as in ach, or as kh. For consistency, this guide favors kh.

31 Which is correct, temple or synagogue?

Contemporary places of worship and study are called by both names, but some reserve the word temple for the original structure. Orthodox Jews do not refer to their houses of worship as temples. Some Conservative and Reconstructionist congregations do. Most Reform congregations use temple as if to say "This is our temple now." Many use neither term, referring instead to a "shul" or a "community." Jewish houses of worship are not called churches.

32 Can you tell whether someone is Jewish by the name?

Many Jews have names that might not sound Jewish and many people with names that might seem Jewish are not. Jews, like non-Jews, have taken surnames from the languages of the countries where they lived. German, Polish or Russian names might sound Jewish because many Jews of those nationalites live in the United States. But many non-Jews have those names, too. Some families of surnames have Jewish roots. They include Cohen (Cohn, Cahn, Kohn, Kahn and more), from the Hebrew word for priest. Another is Levy (Levin, Levine, Levitt and others), from Levi, the biblical tribe. Another Jewish surname is Israel (Israeli, Yisrael, Disraeli). Even some of these names, however, are similar to names that do not have Jewish origins. It is better not to assume someone's identity from their name.

Culture

33 Do Jewish people prefer to keep to themselves?

Most American Jews interact with non-Jewish neighbors, co-workers and friends. Many marry non-Jews. Many Jews seek Jewish neighborhoods for a sense of community. It may or may not have anything to do with being in a place that facilitates religious practices, such as observing the Sabbath or keeping kosher. Still, Jewish people mingle with the world and Jews who are more secular are more likely to live in mixed areas.

34 Why do Orthodox Jews have a distinctive way of dressing?

Modesty is important in Jewish tradition. Orthodox Jewish women wear clothing that is not too bright or tight. Women tend to wear tops with sleeves that cover the elbows and skirts that cover the knees. In some communities, women wear socks, tights or stockings, as well. Clothing laws are not as strict for men, but in some traditions they are discouraged from wearing shorts. Hassidic garb has its roots in historical Eastern European dress. Wearing black can symbolize perpetual readiness for prayer and a lack of concern for color and fashion, allowing one to keep one's priorities straight.

35 What is the significance of the small, circular cap some Jewish men wear?

Wearing a kippah, as it is called in Hebrew, or yarmulke in Yiddish, reminds men that there is someone above them. Some men cover their heads all the time. Some cover their heads only for services, teaching or studying. Others never do.

36 Are there other traditions for men's hair?

Orthodox men have several traditions. One scriptural interpretation says that hair may be trimmed with scissors but not shaved with razors. Electric trimmers, which have blades that do not touch the face, are allowed. Some men choose to wear beards as a sign of their beliefs. Some let sidelocks in front of their ears grow, in keeping with a commandment written in Leviticus that says, "Do not round off (the hair at) the edges of your heads." There are different styles of sidelocks, called "payo" or "payos," from short to long and curled. Some with long sidelocks tuck them behind their ears or under a hat. Some Orthodox Jewish boys have their first haircut at age 3 in a Hassidic celebration called an upshorin.

37 Do Jewish women cover their heads, also?

Women cover their hair after marriage in Orthodox Jewish communities because of a traditional belief that hair is attractive or seductive and should be reserved for husbands. Hair can be covered with hats, scarves or wigs. Some women cover their hair only when entering or praying in a synagogue. Others do not cover their hair at all.

Food

38 What does kosher mean?

The Hebrew noun kashrut encompasses the entire system of keeping kosher. The adjective kosher (pronounced "KO sher" in English and Yiddish and "ka SHARE" in Hebrew) means suitable or fit. It is biblically based. Kosher means that food and places where it is cooked, sold and eaten meet Jewish law. Kosher meat must come from animals that have cloven hooves and chew their cud. This includes cattle, sheep, goats, deer and bison. Pork is not kosher. Fish must have fins and scales, so shellfish like shrimp and lobster are not kosher. Rodents, reptiles, amphibians and insects are forbidden. Animals must be slaughtered in the most humane way possible. Rules include keeping meat and dairy products separate. Foods grown in soil or on plants and bushes are kosher. Food should not be taken from a tree in its first three years.

39 Is kosher for Passover different from regular kosher?

Yes. Food must meet additional requirements to be kosher for Passover. Grains including wheat, spelt (hulled wheat), rye, barley and oats are prohibited unless they are first baked into matzoh under rabbinic supervision. During Passover, most Jews substitute matzoh and foods made from it for cakes, cookies, bread and other products. Rice, millet, corn, dried beans, lentils, peas, green beans, soybeans, peanuts, sesame and poppy seeds and mustard are usually forbidden, at least for Ashkenazic Jews. Before Passover, kitchens are rigorously cleaned to make sure forbidden foods are not present.

40 What is matzoh and its significance?

Matzoh is bread that is unleavened. It is sometimes described as "poor man's bread" or the "bread of affliction" eaten by Israelites enslaved in Egypt. Matzoh symbolizes that Jews had to leave Egypt so quickly they did not have time to let dough rise. Matzoh is thin and crisp and symbolizes faith and trust in God's instructions and his provision of nourishment. It is typically eaten during the Passover holiday.

41 Why do some Jewish people keep kosher while others do not?

This varies by branch and personal practice. Orthodox Jews are obligated to fully obey the dietary requirements of Jewish law. Reform Jews are not required, but may choose to do so. Some Conservative Jews, but not all, observe less stringent requirements, and some do not observe any laws of kashrut.

42 What is challah?

Challah is rich bread made with eggs. It is eaten on Shabbat and on holidays other than Passover. Before meals during these special times, a blessing is said over two loaves of challah to thank God. Two loaves symbolize the two portions of manna given to the children of Israel on the Sabbath's Friday evenings during their exodus from Egypt. Challah is made in several shapes. The most common is the braided challah. It can symbolize love, diversity and unity. During the Jewish new year of Rosh Hashanah, the challah is round, symbolizing the continuation of the cycles of life.

43 What other foods are associated with Jews?

Most Jewish foods reflect places from which people come rather than their religion. Bagels, blintzes, latkes (potato pancakes), corned beef and pastrami sandwiches, chicken soup with matzoh balls and baked puddings called kugels are of Ashkenazic origin. Sephardic and Mizrachic foods are like those of cultures in Spain, Portugal, the Middle East and North Africa. Bourekas, baba ghanoush, hummus, falafel, shawarma and pita reflect Mediterranean cultures.

44 What is the role of wine in Jewish tradition?

Wine symbolizes joy and happiness. Wine is consumed on the Sabbath, holy days and at milestone events such as a circumcision or wedding ceremony. The Passover Seder includes four cups of wine. The wine is usually a sweet grape wine. Grape juice may be substituted.

View video at: http://bit.ly/1ot2yXJ

Demographics

45 What is the Jewish population in the United States?

According to the 2013 American Jewish Year Book, about 5.7 million Jews live in the United States. This is about 2 percent of the U.S. population.

46 What states have the largest Jewish populations?

About a quarter of the country's Jews, 1.6 million, lived in New York according to the 2010 U.S. Census. About 18 percent lived in California. The next eight states in order were Florida, New Jersey, Pennsylvania, Massachusetts, Maryland, Illinois, Ohio and Texas. Jews live in every state.

47 How well do Jews do economically?

In Pew Research's 2013 Portrait of Jewish Americans, 25 percent reported annual household incomes over $150,000, compared with 8 percent of people in the country as a whole. Twenty percent of American

Jews reported household incomes below $30,000 a year. They tended to be younger than 30 or 65 and older.

48 Are Jewish people generous?

According to a 2013 report, about 76 percent of Jews said they made a charitable gift in the prior year. This compared with 63 percent of non-Jews. The difference was greater among households with income below $50,000 a year. Jews were also more likely than the general population to give to social service agencies rather than to their religious congregations, 54 percent compared to 41 percent. The report was by the National Study of American Religious Giving and the National Study of American Jewish Giving.

Where do American Jews live?

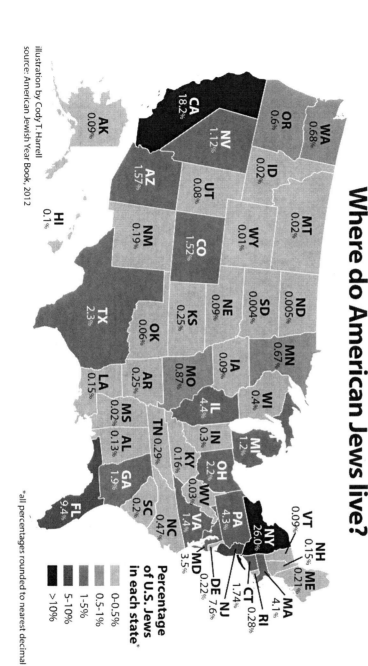

illustration by Cody T. Harrell
source: American Jewish Year Book, 2012

WA 0.68%
OR 0.6%
CA 18.2%
NV 1.12%
AK 0.09%
HI 0.1%
ID 0.02%
UT 0.08%
AZ 1.57%
MT 0.02%
WY 0.01%
CO 1.52%
NM 0.19%
TX 2.3%
ND 0.005%
SD 0.004%
NE 0.09%
KS 0.25%
OK 0.06%
LA 0.15%
AR 0.25%
MO 0.87%
IA 0.09%
MN 0.67%
WI 0.4%
IL 4.4%
MS 0.02%
AL 0.13%
TN 0.29%
GA 1.9%
FL 9.4%
IN 0.3%
KY 0.16%
MI 1.2%
OH 2.2%
WV 0.03%
SC 0.2%
NC 0.47%
VA 1.4%
MD 3.5%
PA 4.3%
DE 0.22%
NJ 7.6%
NY 26.0%
VT 0.09%
NH 0.15%
ME 0.21%
MA 4.1%
CT 1.74%
RI 0.28%

Percentage of U.S. Jews in each state*

0-0.5%
0.5-1%
1-5%
5-10%
>10%

*all percentages rounded to nearest decimal

Population changes

When the Pew Research Center completed the most comprehensive study of the Jewish population in decades in 2013, several trends emerged in regard to Jewish and other religious populations. Below are projected estimates of these populations and the U.S. religious composition from 2010 to 2050.

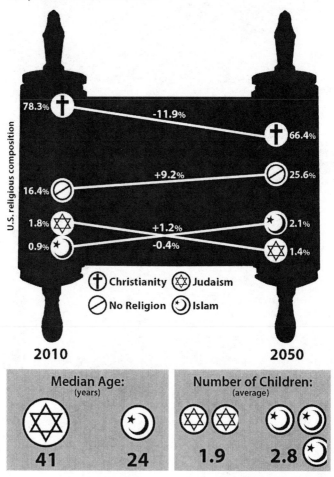

U.S. religious composition

78.3% ✝ -11.9% ✝ 66.4%

16.4% ⊘ +9.2% ⊘ 25.6%

1.8% ✡ +1.2% ☾ 2.1%

0.9% ☾ -0.4% ✡ 1.4%

✝ Christianity ✡ Judaism
⊘ No Religion ☾ Islam

2010   **2050**

Median Age:
(years)

✡ ☾

41   **24**

Number of Children:
(average)

✡✡ ☾☾

1.9   **2.8** ☾

illustration by Cody T. Harrell
source: Pew Research Center, 2013

Family

49 Do Jewish people marry outside their religion?

The Pew Research Center's 2014 Religious Landscape Study reported that 65 percent of Jews who were married or living with a partner were with another Jew. Thirty-five percent said they were living with a non-Jew. A larger Pew study from the year before reported 44 percent of married Jewish respondents were in mixed marriages. The proportion was 58 percent for those who had married since 2005. Pew found practicing Jews are more likely than cultural Jews to marry within the religion.

50 Do most Jewish parents raise their children in the Jewish religion?

That depends largely on whether both parents are Jewish. The 2013 Pew study found that when both parents were Jewish, 96 percent said they were raising their children in the religion. About two-thirds of mixed couples were raising their children to be Jewish to some degree.

51 What is the birth rate for Jewish Americans?

According to the 2013 Pew study, Jewish women aged 40-59 reported having given birth to an average of 1.9 children in their lives. Orthodox women reported an average of 4.1 children. The study indicated that the U.S. Orthodox population is much younger than the general Jewish population. This suggests that the Orthodox proportion of the U.S. Jewish population is growing.

52 What is Judaism's position on birth control?

Jewish people generally are more accepting of contraception than people of other religious groups. This is not true among Orthodox Jews. As with other important matters, the decision depends largely on circumstances and the individual. Jewish teachings value procreation, but do not expressly forbid contraception.

53 What is Judaism's position on abortion?

Jewish views on abortion do not fit easily into the current American yes-or-no debate. Judaism neither bans abortion nor allows for easy and indiscriminate abortion. In general, Jewish law favors the life of the mother over the life of the fetus, but it's rarely an either-or question. A long body of history and many other considerations go into decisions. Most liberal Jews support abortion rights.

Intermarriage is increasing

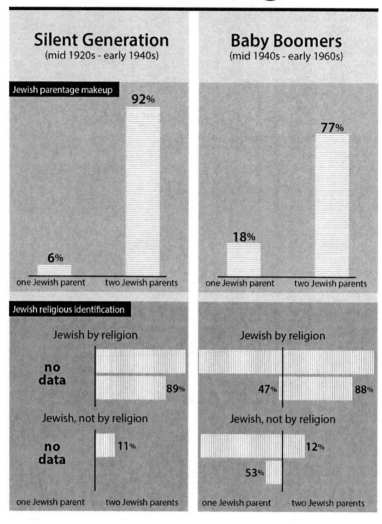

Silent Generation
(mid 1920s - early 1940s)

Jewish parentage makeup

6% one Jewish parent
92% two Jewish parents

Jewish religious identification

Jewish by religion

no data

89%

Jewish, not by religion

no data

11%

one Jewish parent   two Jewish parents

Baby Boomers
(mid 1940s - early 1960s)

18% one Jewish parent
77% two Jewish parents

Jewish by religion

47%   88%

Jewish, not by religion

53%   12%

one Jewish parent   two Jewish parents

illustration by Cody T. Harrell

American Jews have been debating the impact of intermarriage for decades and whether intermarriage diversifies and strengthens the Jewish community as a whole. In 2013, the Pew Research Center looked at intermarriage statistics for the four most recent generations in American history. These charts compare the four periods.

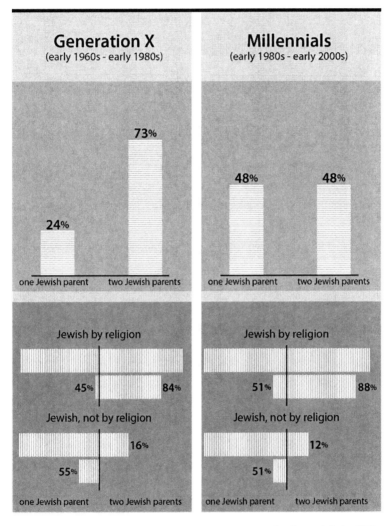

Generation X
(early 1960s - early 1980s)

73%

24%

one Jewish parent   two Jewish parents

Jewish by religion

45%   84%

Jewish, not by religion

16%

55%

one Jewish parent   two Jewish parents

Millennials
(early 1980s - early 2000s)

48%   48%

one Jewish parent   two Jewish parents

Jewish by religion

51%   88%

Jewish, not by religion

12%

51%

one Jewish parent   two Jewish parents

source: Pew Research Center, 2013

Life Cycle

54 Why is circumcision important?

Circumcision is often referred to as the covenant of Abraham, who circumcised himself at God's command when he accepted their relationship. Most Jewish boys are circumcised. This happens at a ceremony called a bris or brit milah, usually on the eighth day after birth. Today, Orthodox and Conservative Jews require male converts to undergo circumcision, or, for those already circumcised, the drawing of a drop of blood. Some Reform rabbis accept converts who do not go through the procedure.

55 What is a mikvah?

Immersion in the mikvah, a specially designed pool of water, is a purifying ritual. The mikvah's most frequent use is by women, especially Orthodox, after their monthly menstrual cycle. Men and women use it before certain holy days, such as the Day of Atonement. It can also be used to symbolize a new beginning. In this context, the mikvah can be used before a wedding, bar or bat mitzvah, or during a conversion ceremony. The mikvah is also used after some life-altering events, such as a birth, miscarriage or divorce. A mikvah must incorporate running water from a natural source, such as a lake or river. Rainwater can be collected and used.

56 What is a bar or bat mitzvah?

Bar or bat mitzvah means "son or daughter of the commandment" and marks the age of 13, or, for Orthodox girls, 12. This is the age of maturity, when people become responsible for performing the commandments. Young people may demonstrate this new status by going before the congregation at the next Shabbat. There, they recite or chant Hebrew blessings, read from the Torah or lead part of the service. Orthodox girls do not participate in regular religious service as boys do. An Orthodox girl might give a commentary on that week's Torah portion or participate in a service with a female congregation. A celebration often accompanies the event. That relatively modern development is optional.

57 In a Jewish wedding, why does the groom break a glass?

The breaking of a glass at the end of a Jewish wedding has many interpretations. One is that it reminds us of the destruction of the Temple. Another is that life includes sorrow or the fragility of marriage. In some weddings, both the bride and the groom stomp on the glass. In all Jewish weddings, you can expect people to cheer "Mazel tov," the Hebrew wish for congratulations or good luck.

58 Does Judaism permit divorce?

Yes. Divorce varies by branch of Judaism. In some streams of Judaism, a bill of divorce, called the "get" is to be given by the husband to grant a divorce. In cases were this is required, women whose husbands refuse to grant a "get" are forbidden from getting remarried.

59 What are Jewish traditions for funerals and burial?

Jewish burials happen soon after death. In the United States, burial usually occurs within three days and before the Sabbath and holy days. Immediately after death a burial society or funeral home will be contacted. The body should never be unattended until burial. No natural or chemical agents may be used to prepare the body. Some have caskets closed at funerals, so as to remember the deceased as they were in life. A rabbi will usually lead prayers and deliver a eulogy. Mourners might place dirt into the grave to symbolize the body decomposing in the ground. A gravestone is usually placed on the burial spot about 11 months after the death.

60 How should guests behave during mourning?

After the burial, family members return to the home for a meal of consolation. This begins the period of mourning, called shiva, which means seven. While mourning traditionally lasts seven days, families today might sit shiva, that is, receive visitors, for only a couple of days. Shiva is required for a father, mother, sister, brother, son, daughter and spouse. During this time, as many as three prayer services may be conducted daily. The synagogue usually ensures that a minyan, at least 10 Jewish adults, is at each service. It is traditional to contribute to charities designated by the family rather than to send flowers. Among traditional Jews, a candle may be burning at the home during shiva. Mirrors might be covered so one is not distracted by personal vanity. After shiva, the family enters a period known as shloshim, which means 30. For 30 days after burial, they refrain from certain types of activities and wear a torn item, which represents mourning. Typically, once the mourning period is over the rent garments are no longer worn. The mourning period for a parent can continue for a year, up until the date of death.

61 Does Judaism permit cremation?

Jewish law requires bodies to be buried. Many consider cremation to be mutilation, which is forbidden. Others feel cremation is an uncomfortable reminder of the Holocaust. While all branches favor burial, cremation is becoming more common for non-Orthodox Jews.

62 What is the position on tattoos and piercings?

Judaism teaches that the body is a gift from God and tattoos were historically seen as a betrayal of this. The Torah says less about piercings. Many Jewish women have pierced ears, but some religious leaders have concerns about multiple piercings. This is not a big religious concern for most modern American Jews.

63 What do Jewish people believe about the afterlife, heaven and hell?

Jewish people have a wide range of beliefs about the afterlife. It is less of a consideration for them than for Christians and Muslims. One view is that we should live to be good people on Earth without regard for reward or punishment later. For some, the lack of proof makes afterlife an irrelevant consideration. Another view is that righteous souls will ascend directly to heaven and evil souls will be kept out until they have achieved atonement.

Gender

64 Is Jewish lineage passed down from the mother or the father?

Conservative and Orthodox Jews recognize a child as Jewish if the mother is Jewish. The Reform Movement's Central Conference of American Rabbis in 1983 recognized children raised in the religion by Jewish fathers or non-Jewish mothers.

65 Can women be rabbis and cantors?

In most streams of Judaism in the United States, this is allowed. It is not allowed among Orthodox Jews. Honorific titles are being added in response to Orthodox feminist activism.

66 Why are women and men separated in Orthodox synagogues?

Prayer is a very important and personal aspect of Judaism. Orthodox Jews believe that separating men and women encourages complete attention to God and not to each other.

67 What does Judaism say about gay rights?

This varies by denomination. The Reform and Reconstructionist movements support gay and lesbian rights and same-sex marriage. The Conservative movement in 2012 approved ceremonies for same-sex couples to marry. Rabbis may choose whether to officiate at these weddings. LGBT Jews can become ordained rabbis in Conservative, Reform and Reconstructionist movements. Orthodox Judaism opposes gay marriage.

Education

68 How educated are American Jews?

Jewish people are one of the nation's most highly educated groups. The proportion of Jewish adults with bachelor's or advanced degrees is double that of the U.S. population overall. About 58 percent of Jewish adults have college degrees, compared with 29 percent of Americans overall according to Pew Research. Jews who reported having a high school education or less were 17 percent, compared with 42 percent of all Americans. Jewish families have historically valued education as a pathway to work and to combat anti-Semitism.

69 What is Hillel?

Hillel is an international organization for Jewish college students. It is active at more than 500 colleges and universities. Its mission is "Enriching the lives of Jewish students so that they may enrich the Jewish people and the world." The name comes from 1st century Rabbi Hillel the Elder, who asked, "If I am not for myself, who will be for me? When I am for myself, what am I? And if not now, when?"

70 What is the Birthright program?

Birthright Israel organizes trips to Israel for 18- to 26-year-olds who have never been there. It is intended to "strengthen bonds with the land and people of Israel and solidarity with Jewish communities worldwide." On a 10-day Birthright trip, participants learn about Israel and the relationship between the land and the Jewish people. The trips are funded by Birthright, the State of Israel, Jewish organizations and philanthropists. Some say Birthright paints a one-sided picture.

71 Are there other educational activities for young Jewish people?

Yes. There are many Jewish day and supplemental after-school and Sunday school programs, often affiliated with synagogues and universities. Many Jewish Americans receive preparation, often in after-school programs, for the bar or bat mitzvah. Religious education can continue through high school. Additionally, there are Jewish study-abroad programs. There are also summer camps affiliated with various denominations and Zionist movements.

Politics

72 Which major political party do Jewish voters support?

In 2014, about 61 percent of people who identified as Jews also identified as Democrats or leaned that way. About 29 percent identified as or leaned toward being Republican. The study, by Gallup, showed that the Democratic preference had declined from 71 percent in 2008. The Democratic preference was higher among women, non-religious Jews and Jews with higher educations.

73 How many members of Congress are Jewish?

In elections for the 2015-2017 Congress, 10 of 100 senators were Jewish and 19 of 445 representatives were Jewish.

74 Is there a Jewish lobby?

There is not an umbrella organization advancing a unified plan for Israel. People who oppose U.S. policy toward Israel sometimes use that stereotype.

Hundreds of non-Jewish business, labor, religious, social and racial groups lobby independently. Jewish lobbying groups operate the same way. Not only do Jewish lobbying groups set their own agendas and campaigns, they often work in opposition.

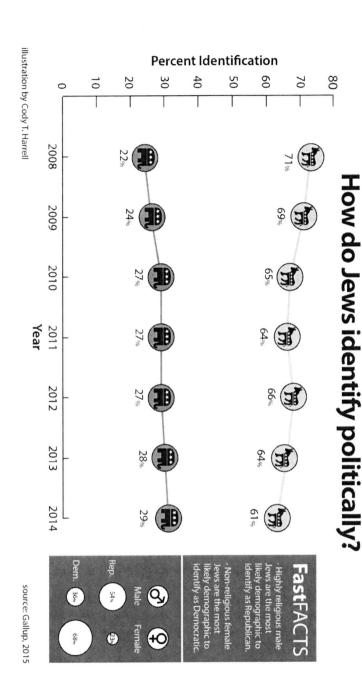

How do Jews identify politically?

Percent Identification

Year

71% 69% 65% 64% 66% 64% 61%

22% 24% 27% 27% 27% 28% 29%

illustration by Cody T. Harrell

FastFACTS

- Highly religious male Jews are the most likely demographic to identify as Republican.

- Non-religious female Jews are the most likely demographic to identify as Democratic.

Male   Female

Rep. 54%   23%

Dem. 36%   68%

source: Gallup, 2015

The Holocaust

75 When and where was the Holocaust?

The Holocaust took place between 1933 and 1945, although the worst part began in 1939. According to the Encyclopedia of the Holocaust, based on research at Yad Vashem, Nazis killed Jews from more than 20 countries in the Holocaust. Most were killed in Europe, particularly Poland, Germany, Ukraine, Lithuania, Hungary, Austria and France. In some countries 90 percent of the Jewish population was killed. All six death camps were in Poland.

76 How many Jews died in the Holocaust?

It is estimated that 6 million or more Jews were killed during the Holocaust. An exact number is difficult to know. Reasons for that include the length of the Holocaust and inconsistency and gaps in records. Research is still going on.

77 Why were Jewish people targeted?

Nazis, under Adolf Hitler, maintained that Germans belonged to a superior race. They identified Jews as a separate race that was a biological threat to this Aryan race. Jews are not a racial group, but include many races, ethnicities and nationalities. Jews were also scapegoated for Germany's defeat in World War I and the depression of the 1930s.

78 Who else was killed in the Holocaust?

Other groups the Nazis considered to be racially inferior were also persecuted and killed. Roma (Gypsies), Sinti, some Slavic and Polish peoples and the disabled were killed. Others were targeted for their views and behavior, rather than presumed racial status. They include communists, socialists, Catholics, Jehovah's Witnesses and gay people. Nobel Peace Prize recipient Elie Wiesel said that while not all victims of the Nazis were Jews, all Jews were victims.

79 How many Holocaust survivors are alive today?

This historically important generation is getting smaller. The registry of survivors of The United States Holocaust Memorial Museum has about 195,000 names. The museum recognizes all people, Jewish or non-Jewish, who were displaced, persecuted or discriminated against during the Holocaust. The registry is voluntary and has members in 59 countries.

80 How is the Holocaust related to the beginnings of modern Israel?

The Holocaust stranded thousands of Jewish refugees in Europe. Most wanted to leave for Palestine, where several hundred thousand Jews were already living, or the United States. In 1948, the United Nations voted to divide Palestine, governed under mandate by the British, into Jewish and Arab states. When Israel became an independent nation in May 1948, it allowed unlimited Jewish immigration.

81 What is a Holocaust denier?

A Holocaust denier says the Holocaust never happened, despite all the witnesses, testimony and evidence. The Anti-Defamation League, The United States Holocaust Memorial Museum and others call denial and distortion forms of anti-Semitism. Deniers are also called revisionists.

82 Have Holocaust survivors received reparations?

Germany has paid money to individuals and to Israel on a number of occasions for a variety of reasons. They include deaths, stolen property and enslavement. In 2014, France agreed to pay $60 million for the French railway's transport of Holocaust victims to Germany and Poland. Some Jews have opposed reparations because they feel there can never be adequate compensation.

Israel

83 What is the biblical relationship of the Jewish people to the land of Israel?

According to the Torah, God told Abraham to leave his homeland. God promised Abraham and his descendants a "land of milk and honey," in Canaan, known today as Israel. Many Jews regard Israel as land promised by God. Through centuries of exile, many Jewish prayers have conveyed a yearning for a return to Zion, or Jerusalem.

84 Why is Jerusalem important to the Jewish people?

The First Temple was built there by King Solomon around 970-931 Before Common Era. An imposing structure, it housed the Ten Commandments inside the Ark of the Covenant. The Babylonians destroyed the Temple in 586 Before Common Era. The tablets with the Commandments and the Ark were lost. Jews returned to the site and built a larger Second Temple in 520-515 Before Common Era. The Romans destroyed that in 70 Common Era. Today, some traditional Jews pray daily for God's restoration of the Temple in Jerusalem.

85 What is the Western Wall?

After the destruction of the Second Temple, a low outer wall remained. As the largest surviving part of the Temple, this became the holiest place for Jews. For centuries, Jews have traveled to pray at the wall. Hearing their prayers, non-Jews called this the "Wailing Wall." Western Wall is preferred.

86 How closely connected do American Jews feel to Israel?

According to Pew's 2013 Portrait of Jewish Americans, 69 percent of respondents who identified as Jews said they felt very or somewhat attached to the Jewish state. Feelings were stronger among Orthodox Jews than among Conservative or Reform Jews.

87 Do Jewish Americans support the policies of Israel?

Just as with U.S. politics, people have varying opinions. Disagreeing with Israeli policies does not mean one does not support the State of Israel. Jewish Americans do not vote in Israel's elections but actively support or oppose its policies.

88 Why are there Israeli flags in some synagogues?

Synagogues have displayed national flags since before the creation of Israel. Most U.S. synagogues that have an Israeli flag display the American flag alongside. The significance of showing national flags in a religious setting is sometimes debated but widely practiced.

89 What is Zionism?

Zionism is the belief that Jews have the right to national self-determination, and that Israel, as the homeland of the Jewish people, has a right to exist. Zion refers to the hill of Jerusalem and represents the historic land of the Jewish people. The World Zionist Organization's congress meets every two years. It decides policy for the Jewish Agency for Israel, which works for the immigration of Jews to Israel. Zionism does not mean an all-Jewish state.

90 How did the modern Zionist movement begin?

Modern Zionism began in the 1880s. Theodor Herzl, a Jewish journalist born in Hungary, noticed the rise of anti-Semitism. He felt a need for a Jewish state and for Jews to return to their ancient land. It is not primarily a religious movement. The World Zionist Organization decided that Palestine, then part of the Ottoman Empire, was the most logical and fitting location for a Jewish state.

Stereotypes

91 What is anti-Semitism?

Anti-Semitism is discriminatory behavior or beliefs against Jewish people. It can be done by individuals or groups. Anti-Semitism is directed at both religious and secular Jews.

92 Where does the word "Semite" come from?

"Semite" initially meant the descendants of Shem, oldest of Noah's three sons. It included people who spoke the Mesopotamian region's languages nearly 3,000 years ago. Today, Semites are people in the Middle East, North Africa, West Asia, or the surrounding region who speak the dialect of their ancestors. This includes Jews, Arabs, Assyrians and others.

93 How did the term become focused on Jewish people?

The term "anti-Semitism" arose in Germany in the 1800s. The "League of Antisemites" used the term to refer exclusively to Jews and to categorize them as a race. The phrase gained currency with the Nazi party in Germany in 1933. Despite the way the label has been narrowed, Jews are not a racial group and include people of every race.

94 How often are hate crimes directed at Jewish people?

Almost two-thirds of 1,340 religious hate crime victims in 2012 were Jews, according to the FBI. Globally, according to a 2015 Pew Report, harassment of Jews was at a seven-year high.

95 Why are Jewish people associated with money?

The association goes back to the Middle Ages. Then, the Catholic Church forbade Christians from taking jobs as moneylenders and barred Jews from jobs other than those in finance. Jews were also forbidden from owning land, which kept them out of farming, the major economy. So, they had to work in trade, business and finance.

96 Do Jewish people control certain industries, such as banking or Hollywood?

This is an old form of anti-Semitism. A 2008 study by the Anti-Defamation League showed that almost 15 percent of nearly 2,000 U.S. residents said Jewish people had too much power on Wall Street. Stereotyping can come from identifying names, sometimes incorrectly, as Jewish and assuming a conspiracy.

97 Are many American Jews also citizens of Israel?

No. One way to undermine people is to question their loyalty. This is behind statements that some Jews are citizens of both the United States and Israel. According to Pew Research almost 90 percent of American Jews surveyed were born in the United States. Others became U.S. citizens. Very few have dual citizenship, and the United States recognizes such arrangements with many countries.

98 Why do Jewish people get blamed for trouble?

For centuries Europeans, who were predominantly Christian, used Jews as scapegoats for their troubles. Problems falsely blamed on Jews included bubonic plague and economic recessions. Adolf Hitler used hatred of Jews to unite Nazi Germany. Scapegoating still happens today and has been growing in countries that oppose Jews or the existence of Israel.

99 What is the Protocols of the Learned Elders of Zion?

This book, written in Russia about 1900, describes a supposed plot by Jews to take over the world. It is a hoax. It is forged from an earlier book about Napoleon III. Hitler often referred to the protocols, and the Nazi Party printed editions of it, as did Henry Ford's "Dearborn Independent" newspaper. The book is still circulated to promote anti-Semitism.

100 What is a "blood libel"?

Historically, a blood libel was the false belief that Jewish people used the blood of Christians, notably children, in religious rites. Although false, thousands were killed in pogroms started by this "blood accusation." Calling other false statements "blood libels" trivializes the term.

Jewish Holidays

By Stephanie Fenton

Year after year, Jewish holidays, festivals, fasts and memorials recall layers of Jewish tradition that extend back through the millennia. The marking of this sacred time still echoes an ancient agricultural society where life depended on changing seasons and observations of natural cycles such as the changing of the moon. Christianity, a faith that came out of Judaism about 2,000 years ago, switched from marking time by lunar cycles to a largely secular calendar. Islam, the third major faith that looks to Abraham as its ancient patriarch, chose to maintain a strictly lunar calendar, so the fasting month of Ramadan eventually cycles through the entire breadth of the modern, secular calendar. Jewish people solved the problem of seasonally drifting holidays by adopting a lunisolar calendar that adjusts the shorter, 12-month lunar calendar by adding a leap month in the spring every two or three years. This keeps holidays in sync with the natural cycles of the Earth. For example, the main Jewish New Year is the beginning of the High Holidays, which consist of the New Year and Day of Atonement. They always occur in September or October and are part of the High Holidays and the joyous Sukkot harvest festival that concludes this spiritually intense period.

Nissan is the first month in the Jewish ecclesiastical calendar and Passover occurs on 15 Nissan. The date is fixed on the Jewish calendar but varies on the secular calendar.

American Jews vary widely in their levels of observance. Some observe dietary kosher laws; some don't. Some observe every Jewish holiday and festival; others observe the major holidays.

This guide will help you appreciate the relative importance of the major and minor Jewish observances as well as the newer holidays that have been added since the establishment of the State of Israel in 1948. In Judaism, a day begins at sunset. Work is not permitted on Shabbat and the following holidays: Rosh Hashanah, Yom Kippur, Sukkot, Shemini Atzeret (the end of Sukkot), Simchat Torah, Passover and Shavuot. During Passover, Jews refrain from work on the first, second, seventh and eighth days.

This is an overview starting at the beginning of the Jewish year. It includes some of the important Jewish observances you might encounter in a religiously diverse community of friends, neighbors and co-workers.

Which holidays do Jews consider to be most important?

The Public Religion Research Institute conducted a Jewish Values survey in 2012 to learn more about the values of both observant Jews and ancestral Jews. Survey respondents were asked to identify which Jewish holiday they considered to be most important.

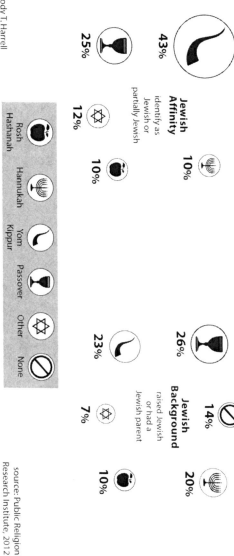

Jewish Affinity
identify as Jewish or partially Jewish

43%
25%
12%
10%
10%
14%

Jewish Background
raised Jewish or had a Jewish parent

26%
23%
7%
10%
20%

Rosh Hashanah | Hannukah | Yom Kippur | Passover | Other | None

illustration by Cody T. Harrell

source: Public Religion Research Institute, 2012

Rosh Hashanah (Jewish New Year)

If you hear someone referring to the Jewish New Year, they're talking about the major holiday of Rosh Hashanah, translated as "Head of the Year." On 1 Tishrei as Rosh Hashanah begins, the Jewish calendar advances to the next year. Jews regularly adjust their lunisolar calendar to keep the holidays roughly in the same seasons—so this Jewish New Year moves around but always lands between Sept. 5 and Oct. 5. Jews refrain from work during this two-day festival. Friends wish each other a sweet new year and consume honey, from a popular dip for apples to many kinds of treats and pastries. Rosh Hashanah also begins the High Holidays, a period of reflection on the past year and hopes for the year ahead. Jews have 10 days from Rosh Hashanah until Yom Kippur to seek forgiveness and reconciliation with relatives, friends and co-workers.

View video at: http://bit.ly/1ot2yXR

The blowing of the shofar, a ram's horn trumpet, is associated both with Rosh Hashanah and Yom Kippur.

Yom Kippur (Day of Atonement)

Often described as the holiest day of the Jewish year, Yom Kippur is the Day of Atonement on 10 Tishrei—a 25-hour period of fasting, intense prayer, liturgies in the synagogue and repentance. There are many historical and spiritual layers to this daylong holiday. Here is one way Yom Kippur often is described: Jews have asked forgiveness and sought reconciliation with others prior to this holy day. Then, they gather in communities on Yom Kippur to seek forgiveness and reconciliation with God in preparation for the new year now unfolding.

Sukkot (Feast of Tabernacles)

For Sukkot, which begins on 15 Tishrei, it is traditional to build a temporary structure, called a sukkah in Hebrew, to dwell in during the seven-day festival. These structures, which include a loosely thatched roof that allows families to glimpse the stars, are reminders of temporary shelters used by ancestors. During Sukkot, families have their meals inside the sukkah. Some even try to sleep in it. This is a festive time when friends and relatives visit each other, share stories and enjoy the meal. Prayers during Sukkot involve symbols reminiscent of ancestors who were more dependent on agriculture. A daily practice during Sukkot involves four species of plants: branches of the palm, the myrtle and the willow, and the etrog, a citron that is a big, bumpy cousin to modern lemons. The first three kinds are bound together into a lulav. Then, the lulav and the etrog are shaken together three times in six directions: south, north, east, west, up and down. This is accompanied by a prayer that blessings be drawn from the corners of the Earth and sent back throughout creation.

Shemini Atzeret

Shemini Atzeret is the eighth day of Sukkot. It is on 22 Tishrei. One ancient practice on this holiday is a prayer for rain.

Simchat Torah

This holiday on 23 Tishrei marks the end of one annual cycle of Torah readings and the immediate beginning of another. Congregations try to make this an event for the entire family, including a parade with Torah scrolls featuring volunteer scroll-bearers dancing as they move among the congregation.

Hanukkah (Festival of Lights)

One of the holidays most familiar outside of Judaism, Hanukkah has gained more importance in the United States than it actually holds in the Jewish calendar. Each year, American Jewish leaders emphasize: "Hanukkah is not the Jewish Christmas." However, commercial messages and popular culture encourage gift giving during Hanukkah much like gift giving for Christmas. The annual friction of these holidays in public places has become known as the "December dilemma." The original significance of the eight-day festival, which begins on 25 Kislev, recalls a dire threat to Judaism more than 2,000 years ago. The Temple was desecrated and the future of Judaism was threatened. Then, a group called the Maccabees led a triumphant fight to reclaim and re-dedicate the Temple. As candles are lit today and displayed near windows in Jewish homes, stories are told about a miraculous quantity of sacred oil that seemed too small when the Temple was re-dedicated but burned for eight nights. Today, American Jews describe the holiday as a celebration of religious freedom as they remember their ancestors in Israel heroically struggling to preserve their traditions for future generations.

Tu B'Shvat (New Year for Trees)

Tu B'Shvat is the 15th day of the month of Shvat, which gives the holiday its name. This minor holiday is one of four "new years" and usually occurs in January or February of the secular calendar. In the ancient world, it was important to mark the age of food-producing trees for tithing. Today, Jewish communities celebrate Tu B'Shvat with events encouraging environmental awareness.

Purim

The jubilant major holiday of Purim on the Jewish date of 14 Adar focuses on the story of Queen Esther, who courageously stood up for her people and saved many Jewish lives as a result. In synagogue, the Book of Esther is read. In Jewish communities, Purim is celebrated with merriment, noisemakers, sweets and costumes. Children re-enact the story, often playing the main characters in the Esther story—including the evil Haman and the good Mordechai—in full costume and with robust input from the audience. A Purim meal usually includes plenty of alcohol for the adults—and triangular-shaped, fruit-filled cookies called hamentaschen in Yiddish, or "Haman's pockets."

Pesach (Passover)

Passover is the most widely observed Jewish holiday. For eight days, starting with 15 Nissan, Passover recalls the ancient Israelites' Exodus from slavery in Egypt. During Passover, Jewish families are reminded of when they were slaves in Egypt. Prior to the start of Passover, it is traditional for observant Jews to clean their homes so that not even a crumb of leavened food, or chametz, is present. While only one Seder is conducted in Israel, outside of Israel the first two nights of Passover have a Seder—a meal with symbolic foods, prayers, stories, songs and activities. In some homes, the Seder can last deep into the night. Most Jewish communities also offer "model Seders" for non-Jews who want to learn about this experience prior to Passover. Many non-Jews are familiar from movies and TV shows with some of the Passover customs, such as the moment when the youngest in the household asks Four Questions, beginning with: "Why is this night different from all other nights?" Passover usually is experienced as a family reunion, a history lesson, an affirmation of survival and a time of reflecting on ways to help the vulnerable.

Yom HaShoah (Holocaust Remembrance Day)

Yom HaShoah is a remembrance day, established in Israel in 1953 to remember the 6 million Jews who were killed in the Holocaust, also known as the Shoah. In English, its full title is Holocaust and Heroism Remembrance Day. It is observed on 27 Nissan, the Jewish date of the anniversary of the Warsaw Ghetto uprising in World War II. On the morning of Yom HaShoah, a siren sounds in Israel and all movement stops, including bicycles and cars. In 2005, the United Nations added an International Holocaust Remembrance Day each Jan. 27, the anniversary of the liberation of Auschwitz-Birkenau in 1945. Now, many American Jews mark both dates. While no specific religious customs are mandated, community programs of remembrance often are organized.

Yom Hazikaron (Day of Remembrance for the Fallen Soldiers of Israel and Victims of Terrorism)

Yom Ha'atzmaut (Israeli Independence Day)

Yom Hazikaron is Israeli Memorial Day on 4 Iyar, established in 1963. In English, the full title of this observance is: Day of Remembrance for the Fallen Soldiers of Israel and Victims of Terrorism. The next day, 5 Iyar, is Yom Ha'atzmaut or Israeli Independence Day. In Israel, these are key events, just as Americans mark Memorial Day and the Fourth of July. The first of the two Israeli holidays is solemn; the second day's expression is jubilant. In the rest of the world, Jewish communities often organize public events.

Lag BaOmer

Lag BaOmer is a joyous holiday that occurs on 18 Iyar and recalls a number of milestones in Jewish history. In Israel and in some American Jewish communities, bonfires are a nighttime custom.

Yom Yerushalayim (Jerusalem Day)

Jerusalem Day on 28 Iyar is another modern holiday. It commemorates the 1967 reunification of Jerusalem under Israeli control, during the Six-Day War. Parades in Jerusalem and festive music and readings mark the holiday.

Shavuot (Festival of Weeks)

On 6 Sivan, Jews celebrate the major, ancient holiday of Shavuot to celebrate receiving the Torah. Shavuot is usually a time for joyous meals and alternatively is known as the Festival of First Fruits. Thousands of years ago, Shavuot was a time when families harvested first crops and brought them to the Temple. At Shavuot, the Book of Ruth is read. Some Jews may follow the custom of trying to stay awake all night in study of the Torah.

Tisha B'Av

A major fast day, Tisha B'Av (or, the Ninth of Av) is a time of mourning a number of tragedies that have befallen the Jewish people. According to Jewish teaching, both the First Temple and the Second Temple were destroyed on 9 Av. This is a 25-hour fast and includes prohibitions on bathing, anointing and the wearing of leather shoes. Observant Jews might choose not to work on this day because they are studying and fasting. Jewish congregations place black drapings around the ark, where Torah scrolls are kept. In synagogues, the Book of Lamentations is read.

A former editor with the Detroit area's Suburban Lifestyles Community Newspapers, Stephanie Fenton covered religion for AnnArbor.com. Since 2007, she has provided the nation's only daily coverage of religious holidays, festivals and milestones for ReadTheSpirit online magazine and publishing company.

Epilogue

One hundred questions cannot do justice to millennia of history. They are but a small start. We hope this guide gives you confidence to continue that journey. As you know by now, while the Jewish people have a shared heritage and experience, individual experiences and practices vary widely. Keep in mind that one person's story is not the story of all Jewish people. Many are happy to answer questions. Even if the question is not stated the best way, sincere interest and an open mind can lead to a rich conversation.

Questioning is such a part of Jewish learning and tradition that honest exploration is appreciated. But, as Rabbi Bob Alper explains in his foreword, don't expect consensus answers. Instead, expect to find that people look at situations and beliefs from every point of view, respecting others' rights to their own opinions.

With this in mind, we asked many people to check our work. All of our expert allies suggested meaningful changes. Many asked us to talk to others to get their perspectives, too. They did not always agree, but there was always respect. The editing felt like being supported by a circle of people working together for the best result. One ally, Judy Loebl, said that she tells the people she teaches, "If you come out of here with more questions than answers, we've done our job." The idea is for her learners and for our readers to keep exploring.

Besides talking with a number of people, there is much to be learned as a guest at a Jewish service or home. Take advantage of such invitations or, if you are adventurous, ask for them. Some things are better learned by observation than by reading or discussion.

We will leave you with some resources here and if you spend very much time looking around, you will find that Jewish organizations have put a tremendous amount of material online and in print. In making this guide, we relied on some of that material and, as we often do in this series, work by the Pew Research Center. The guide is certainly in no way better than what you will find from Jewish sources, so we see our mission as little more than pointing you in their direction. If what you have read has been intriguing or enlightening, don't stop now! There is so much more to learn.

Glossary

brakha: Hebrew for a blessing. The plural form is berakhot. Blessings are recited for significant occasions such as putting on the prayer shawl or finishing a meal. The after-meal prayers are called Birkat HaMazon and are a series of blessings that are sung or said.

chai: A Hebrew word that symbolizes life, it is pronounced "khy." The Jewish numerological values of its letters, het and yud, add up to 18. For this reason, gifts of money at weddings and other celebrations are made in multiples of 18 to signify a good life. The word is sometimes worn as jewelry.

chametz: Any food made from leavened grain, forbidden during Passover.

dreidel: A four-sided top spun by children and adults during Hanukkah. Each side has a Hebrew letter. In the Diaspora, outside of Israel, the letters are nun, gimel, hay and shin. Together, the letters stand for "a great miracle happened there." Inside Israel, a dreidel has the letter pe instead of shin and means "a great miracle happened here."

gentile: Someone who is not Jewish.

get: A procedure or the paperwork for a legal Jewish divorce.

gelt: Yiddish for money, this refers to the chocolate coins that are prizes when spinning the dreidel at Hanukkah.

halakha: The body of Jewish law, derived from the Torah.

hora: A traditional Jewish dance to songs such as Havah Nagila in which people join in a circle.

Kabbalat Shabbat: A service that precedes the regular evening prayer on Friday and welcomes the Shabbat.

kashrut: The body of Judaic dietary laws.

mazel tov: This translates as "good luck," and a call for blessings. It often is used to express congratulations for happy events.

mitzvah: One of the 613 commandments. The mitzvahs are divided into two categories, 365 negative commandments, which correspond to the number of days in the year, and 248 positive commandments, corresponding to 248 limbs in the body. According to the Talmud, these are all the moral laws. The word mitzvah is also used to mean a good deed.

Shabbat: The Sabbath, from sunset Friday to sunset Saturday.

shalom: It means peace, prosperity, completeness. It can be used for hello or goodbye.

shul: This means school, but almost always designates a synagogue.

tefillah: Prayer. This can be ancient or modern words from a prayer book or an extemporaneous prayer.

Sacred Objects

aron kodesh: The ark or holy cabinet where Torahs are stored.

chuppah: The four-cornered tapestry that a Jewish couple stands under during their wedding.

ketubah: The contract the bride and groom sign before the wedding. It details each partner's responsibilities.

menorah: One of the oldest symbols of the Jewish religion, this is a seven-branched candelabrum. During Hanukkah, a nine-branched candleholder called a Chanukiah or Chunikiah menorah is used. Eight branches represent the number of days that legend says one day's quantity of oil lasted at the rededication of the Temple in Jerusalem. The ninth spot, which should not be in line with the other eight, holds a candle used for lighting the other candles.

mezuzah: A small piece of parchment with a biblical passage, held in a cylindrical or rectangular container. The container is mounted on the doorway into a home or office to symbolize God's watchfulness.

ner tamid: The eternal light that glows above the ark in every synagogue. It represents the eternal flame that was in the tent of meeting and later the Temple in Jerusalem.

shofar: A ram's horn blown on Rosh Hashanah and Yom Kippur.

siddur: Jewish prayer book consisting of daily prayers.

Star of David: A symbol of Judaism that has become relevant in the Jewish religion only over the past few hundred years. The six-pointed Star of David is on Israel's flag.

tallit: A fringed prayer shawl worn during morning service. Men historically wore these, but women have started to wear them, too. A prayer leader may wear one at evening and morning services.

tefillin: Some observant Jewish men and, less commonly, women, wear these leather boxes for weekday morning prayers. The boxes contain small pieces of parchment with verses of the Torah. They are worn as reminders that God brought the children of Israel out of Egypt. The arm box, called shel yad, goes on the upper arm and the leather strap is wrapped around the arm, hand and fingers. The shel rosh is placed above the forehead.

tzitzit: Knotted fringes that are attached to the four corners of the tallit. Some Orthodox men wear tzitzit all the time attached to an undershirt called a tallit katan. The fringes are a reminder of God's 613 commandments.

yad: Yad means hand and refers to a finger-shaped pointer that is used with the Torah so readers can keep their place without touching and damaging the scroll.

Resources

Blech, Benjamin. *The Complete Idiot's Guide to Understanding Judaism*. 2d ed. Indianapolis: Alpha Books, 2003. Print.

Diamant, Anita, and Howard Cooper. *Living a Jewish Life, Updated and Revised Edition: Jewish Traditions, Customs, and Values for Today's Families*. New York: William Morrow Paperbacks, 2007. Print.

Fermaglich, Kirsten. *American Dreams and Nazi Nightmares: Early Holocaust Consciousness and Liberal America, 1957-1965*. Waltham: Brandeis, 2006. Print.

Goldberg, Andrew, director. *Jerusalem: Center of the World*. PBS: 2009. Video.

Goldstein, Eric L. *The Price of Whiteness: Jews, Race, and American Identity*. Princeton: Princeton University Press, 2008. Print.

Gurock, Jeffrey S. *Orthodox Jews in America (The Modern Jewish Experience)*. Bloomington: Indiana University Press, 2009. Print.

Kolatch, Alfred J. *Inside Judaism: The Concepts, Customs, And Celebrations of the Jewish People*. New York: Jonathan David Publishers, 2006. Print.

Kolatch, Alfred J. *The Jewish Book of Why* (2 vols). Revised. London: Penguin Books, 2003. Print.

Kukoff, Lydia. *Introduction to Judaism: A Source Book*. Revised. New York: URJ Press, 1999. Print.

Lupovitch, Howard N. *Jews and Judaism in World History*. London: Routledge, 2010. Print.

Matlins, Stuart M., and Arthur J. Magida (eds.). *How to Be a Perfect Stranger, 6th Edition: The Essential Religious Etiquette Handbook*. Woodstock: SkyLight Paths, 2015. Print.

Matlins, Stuart M. *The Perfect Stranger's Guide to Funerals and Grieving Practices: A Guide to Etiquette in Other People's Religious Ceremonies*. Woodstock: SkyLight Paths, 2000. Print.

Moffic, Evan. *What Every Christian Needs to Know about Passover: What It Means and Why It Matters*. Nashville: Abingdon Press, 2015. Print.

Robinson, George. *Essential Judaism: A Complete Guide to Beliefs, Customs & Rituals*. New York: Atria Books, 2001. Print.

Schama, Simon. *The Story of the Jews* (2 vols.). New York: Ecco, 2014 and 2015. Print, with accompanying PBS video of same title.

Sonsino, Rifat, and Daniel B. Syme. *Finding God: Selected Responses*. New York: URJ Press, 2002. Print.

Sonsino, Rifat, and Daniel B. Syme. *What Happens After I Die? Jewish Views of Life After Death*. New York: URJ Press, 1990. Print.

Spitz, Elie Kaplan. *Does the Soul Survive? A Jewish Journey to Belief in Afterlife, Past Lives & Living with Purpose*. Woodstock: Jewish Lights, 2001. Print.

Syme, Daniel B. and Cindy Frenkel Kanter. *100 Essential Books for Jewish Readers*. New York: Citadel, 2000.

Syme, Daniel B. *The Jewish Home: A Guide for Jewish Living*. Revised. New York: URJ Press, 2003. Print.

Telushkin, Joseph. *Jewish Literacy Revised Ed: The Most Important Things to Know About the Jewish Religion, its People, and its History.* New York: William Morrow Paperbacks, 2008. Print.

Online Resources

Bureau of Jewish Education. Encyclopedia Judaica. http://www.bjeindy.org/resources/library/encyclopediajudaica/ Online.

Jewish Values Online, http://www.jewishvaluesonline.org/

Jewish Women: A Comprehensive Historical Encyclopedia (Jewish Women's Archive), http://jwa.org/encyclopedia

My Jewish Learning, http://www.myjewishlearning.com/

Navigating the Bible (weekly readings from the Torah and the Prophets), http://bible.ort.org/

Patheos, http://www.patheos.com/Library/Judaism.html

Pew Research Center on Religion & Public Life, http://www.pewforum.org/

USC Shoah Foundation Visual History Archive (Holocaust testimonies), https://sfi.usc.edu/vha

Voice/Vision Holocaust Survivor Oral History Archive (Michigan survivors), http://holocaust.umd.umich.edu/

Yiddish Book Center, http://www.yiddishbookcenter.org/

Organizations

American Israel Public Affairs Committee, www.
aipac.org

American Jewish Committee, http://www.ajc.org

American Jewish World Service, http://www.ajws.
org

Anti-Defamation League, http://www.adl.org/

BBYO teen leadership organization, http://bbyo.org/

Big Tent Judaism, http://bigtentjudaism.org/

Birthright Israel of North America, Inc., www.
birthrightisrael.com

B'nai Brith International, http://www.bnaibrith.org/

Chabad, http://www.chabad.org/

Hadassah. The Women's Zionist Organization of
America, http://www.hadassah.org/

Hillel International, http://www.hillel.org/

Holocaust Memorial Center, http://www.
holocaustcenter.org/

Interfaith Family, http://www.interfaithfamily.com/

JCC Maccabi Games, http://www.jccmaccabigames.
org/

Jewish Community Centers Association of North
America, http://www.jcca.org

Jewish Federations of North America, www.
jewishfederations.org

Jewish Reconstructionist Communities, www.
jewishrecon.org

Jewish Voice for Peace, https://jewishvoiceforpeace.org/

JStreet, jstreet.org

Keshet (LGBT), http://www.keshetonline.org/

NCSY (Orthodox Union youth), https://ncsy.org/

NFTY (Reform youth), http://www.nfty.org/

Orthodox Union, www.ou.org

Society for Humanistic Judaism, http://www.shj.org/

Union for Reform Judaism, http://www.urj.org/

United Synagogue of Conservative Judaism, http://www.uscj.org

United Synagogue Youth, http://www.usy.org/

U.S. Holocaust Memorial Museum, http://www.ushmm.org

World Jewish Congress, http://www.worldjewishcongress.org

World Zionist Organization/American Section, http://www.wzo.org.il

Yad Vashem: The Holocaust Martyrs' and Heroes' Remembrance Authority, http://www.yadvashem.org/

News

Detroit Jewish News, http://www.thejewishnews.com/

The Forward. Forward.com

JTA Jewish Telegraphic Agency, www.jta.org

Our Story

The 100 Questions and Answers series springs from the idea that good journalism should increase cross-cultural competence and understanding. Most of our guides are created by Michigan State University journalism students.

We use journalistic interviews to surface the simple, everyday questions that people have about each other but might be afraid to ask. We use research and reporting to get the answers and then put them where people can find them, read them and learn about each other.

These cultural competence guides are meant to be conversation starters. We want people to use these guides to get some baseline understanding and to feel comfortable asking more questions. We put a resources section in every guide we make and we arrange community conversations. While the guides can answer questions in private, they are meant to spark discussions.

Making these has taught us that people are not that different from each other. People share more similarities than differences. We all want the same things for ourselves and for our families. We want to be accepted, respected and understood.

Please email your thoughts and suggestions to Series Editor Joe Grimm at joe.grimm@gmail.com, at the Michigan State University School of Journalism.

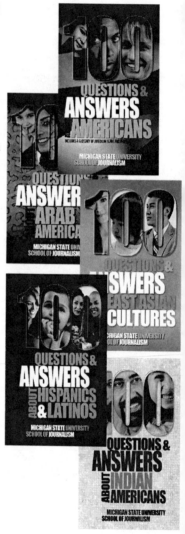

http://news.jrn.msu.edu/culturalcompetence

Related Books

100 Questions and Answers About Americans
Michigan State University School of Journalism, 2013
This guide answers some of the first questions asked by
newcomers to the United States. Questions represent
dozens of nationalities coming from Africa, Asia,
Australia, Europe and North and South America. Good
for international students, guests and new immigrants.
http://news.jrn.msu.edu/culturalcompetence/

ISBN: 978-1-939880-20-8

100 Questions and Answers About Arab Americans
Michigan State University School of Journalism, 2014
The terror attacks of Sept. 11, 2001, propelled these Americans into a difficult position where they are victimized
twice. The guide addresses stereotypes, bias and misin-
formation. Key subjects are origins, religion, language
and customs. A map shows places of national origin.
http://news.jrn.msu.edu/culturalcompetence/

ISBN: 978-1-939880-56-7

100 Questions and Answers About East Asian Cultures
Michigan State University School of Journalism, 2014
Large university enrollments from Asia prompted
this guide as an aid for understanding cultural differences. The focus is on people from China, Japan,
Korea and Taiwan and includes Mongolia, Hong
Kong and Macau. The guide includes history, language, values, religion, foods and more.
http://news.jrn.msu.edu/culturalcompetence/

ISBN: 978-939880-50-5

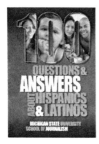

100 Questions and Answers About Hispanics & Latinos
Michigan State University School of Journalism, 2014
This group became the largest ethnic minority in the
United States in 2014 and this guide answers many of
the basic questions about it. Questions were suggested
by Hispanics and Latinos. Includes maps and charts
on origin and size of various Hispanic populations.
http://news.jrn.msu.edu/culturalcompetence/

ISBN: 978-1-939880-44-4

Print and ebooks available on Amazon.com and other retailers.

Related Books

100 Questions and Answers About Indian Americans
Michigan State University School of Journalism, 2013
In answering questions about Indian Americans, this guide also addresses Pakistanis, Bangladeshis and others from South Asia. The guide covers religion, issues of history, colonization and national partitioning, offshoring and immigration, income, education, language and family.
http://news.jrn.msu.edu/culturalcompetence/

ISBN: 978-1-939880-00-0 m

100 Questions, 500 Nations: A Guide to Native America
Michigan State University School of Journalism, 2014
This guide was created in partnership with the Native American Journalists Association. The guide covers tribal sovereignty, treaties and gaming, in addition to answers about population, religion, U.S. policies and politics. The guide includes the list of federally recognized tribes.
http://news.jrn.msu.edu/culturalcompetence/

ISBN: 978-1-939880-38-3

100 Questions and Answers About Veterans
Michigan State University School of Journalism, 2015
This guide treats the more than 20 million U.S. military veterans as a cultural group with distinctive training, experiences and jargon. Graphics depict attitudes, adjustment challenges, rank, income and demographics. Includes six video interviews by Detroit Public Television.
http://news.jrn.msu.edu/culturalcompetence/

ISBN: 978-1-942011-00-2

100 Questions and Answers About American Jews
We begin by asking and answering what it means to be Jewish in America. The answers to these wide-ranging, base-level questions will ground most people and set them up for meaningful conversations with Jewish acquaintances. We cover matters of faith, food, culture, politics and stereotypes.
http://news.jrn.msu.edu/culturalcompetence/

ISBN: 978-1-942011-22-4

Print and ebooks available on Amazon.com and other retailers.

Related Books

100 Questions and Answers About Muslim Americans
Michigan State University School of Journalism, 2014
This guide was done at a time of rising intolerance in the United States toward Muslims. The guide describes the presence of this religious group around the world and inside the United States. It includes audio on how to pronounce some basic Muslim words.
http://news.jrn.msu.edu/culturalcompetence/

ISBN: 978-1-939880-79-6

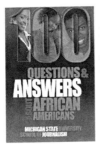

100 Questions and Answers About African Americans
Michigan State University School of Journalism, 2016
Learn about the racial issues that W.E.B. DuBois said in 1900 would be the big challenge for the 20th century. This guide explores Black and African American identity, history, language, contributions and more. Learn more about current issues in American cities and campuses.
http://news.jrn.msu.edu/culturalcompetence/

ISBN: 978-1-942011-19-4

The New Bullying
THE NEW BULLYING Bullying has changed considerably. This book is intended to document that change. Among the changes that were examined are the rise of cyberbullying, social exclusion as a form of bullying, new laws about school bullying, computer crimes and threats and a growing willingness on the part of the public to talk about bullying and its perceived connection to suicide and violence, especially in schools.

ISBN: 978-1-934879-63-4

Print and ebooks available on Amazon.com and other retailers.

CPSIA information can be obtained
at www.ICGtesting.com
Printed in the USA
FFOW03n2308030416
22868FF

9 781942 011224